The Mu...

LITTLE GUIDE TO

BIG

MOTIVATION

RUTH MEINTS

All the students and parents represented in this book are a montage of personalities I've encountered in my studio over the last thirty five years of teaching. All names of students and parents have been changed.

Text: Ruth Meints
Back Cover Photo: May Yap Photography
Cover Design: Danielle Smith-Boldt
Interior Design & Layout: Danielle Smith-Boldt

ISBN: 978-1-736-99410-8

DEDICATION

To my incredible husband Ken and our three boys,
Skyler, Aldric, and Dryden.

ACKNOWLEDGMENTS

I would like to thank my husband Ken and my three sons for all their support in all the things! I'm grateful for all the students and families I have had the honor of working with over the last thirty five years. Special thanks to the Omaha Conservatory of Music for being such a special place to teach, perform, and enjoy music. A big thank you to Candace Jorgensen for her commitment to excellence in music education and the String Sprouts curriculum. Thank you to Mr. John Kendall, my mentor and teacher who demonstrated clearly through his inspired teaching how to meet every student exactly where they were in their learning process.

Thank you to Pasha Sabouri and Chad Peevy for supporting me through the challenge of writing a book. I am so grateful to Liz Huett for her expert editing and advice, as well as Danielle Smith-Boldt for guiding me through the layout, design, and publishing process.

A huge thank you to author and educator Richard Lavoie who motivated me to think about motivation in my studio in a whole new way!

TABLE OF CONTENTS

FOREWORD

by Richard Lavoie

I remember conferencing with a teacher about an unmotivated student. The boy was struggling mightily in her class and she cited his lack of motivation as a sole reason for his failure.

She was not responding well to my suggestion that perhaps SHE could make changes in her approach rather than expecting the struggling child to make all the necessary adjustments.

After a prolonged and fruitless discussion, I finally blurted out "Most kids don't come with batteries included… The teacher has to put the batteries in!"

To my mind a teacher who says, "This child is not learning because he's not motivated" is akin to a car salesman saying to his manager, "I didn't sell any cars this week because I didn't have any motivated buyers."

The job of the salesman is to motivate the buyer. The job of the teacher is to motivate the student. Full stop.

Student motivation is Job #1. This is true for teachers, therapist, coaches...and music instructors.

I have been preaching this truth across the country for forty years and I am constantly amazed and puzzled by the fact that most teachers simply do not understand the basics of student motivation. Further, most teachers subscribe to basic misconceptions about the nature of motivation.

Primary among these dangerous myths are:

"The student is totally unmotivated." and

"The student is simply lazy."

Actually there is no such thing as an unmotivated child because EVERY HUMAN BEHAVIOR IS MOTIVATED. If the child chooses to skip your music lesson, he is not unmotivated...he is motivated to skip your lesson. And your job is to find out 'why' and do what you can to eliminate the toxic element.

The charge of laziness is often leveled against a child when the true cause is actually learned helplessness. Countless studies prove the fact that, if a child feels that the goal is unattainable, he simply stops trying.

Ruth Meints' *The Music Teacher's Little Guide To Big Motivation* explodes these myths and provides the music teacher with concrete strategies that can be used in any music classroom or studio.

Ruth generously acknowledges my work in her introduction. My theories and philosophies have been used by coaches, therapists and teachers in settings as diverse as suburban nursery schools and prison populations.

But I have never–ever–seen my theories applied with such creativity, innovation and vision. The readable, user-friendly format and her specific anecdotes and examples clearly demonstrate her knowledge of and sensitivity for music students... and the good folks to provide them with the gift of music.

Any music instructor would benefit from Ruth's wisdom. If you are a music teacher, use this book. If you KNOW a music teacher, gift them with this book. It is truly a game changer that will add excitement, enthusiasm, and effectiveness to your lessons.

With every good wish,

Rick Lavoie

Author, *The Motivation Breakthrough*

rick@ricklavoie.com

INTRODUCTION

In 1911, a man named Edward Thorndike came up with the Law of Effect. If it weren't so obvious, we might all gasp in admiration at the brilliance of the finding. In case you missed it, here is Thorndike's own explanation from his book *Animal Intelligence:*

> *The Law of Effect is that: Of several responses made to the same situation, those which are accompanied or closely followed by satisfaction to the animal will, other things being equal, be more firmly connected with the situation, so that, when it recurs, they will be more likely to recur; those which are accompanied or closely followed by discomfort to the animal will, other things being equal, have their connections with that situation weakened, so that, when it recurs, they will be less likely to occur. The greater the satisfaction or discomfort, the greater the strengthening or weakening of the bond.*

In other words, the more satisfaction that is gained from engaging in a particular behavior, the more likely that behavior is to be repeated. Conversely, behaviors that result in a negative or unpleasant experience are likely to occur less frequently.

I did, in fact, gasp inwardly when I heard this law for the first time, because it was such an obvious truth, which had been confirmed many times over by the motivation levels of my very own students and their interest in practicing...or lack thereof. I had always valued "having fun" in the lesson, because, in general, I noticed that when students were having fun, they learned more quickly and definitely seemed to practice more between lessons.

Even though the Law of Effect is such a no-brainer, I found myself easily forgetting about it. How do I know this? The answer is simple: unmotivated students. I've been a violin and viola teacher for over 30 years, and I must confess that it often feels like I'm in the business of motivating rather than teaching music. Basically, I realized that I could be the most phenomenal teacher on planet Earth, but if I couldn't motivate my students to practice, I was sunk. As soon as I realized this, I became obsessed with developing some real tools for motivating young musicians to achieve their potential.

The key to successfully motivating anyone to do anything was right there, staring me in the face, in the Law of Effect. If practicing was satisfying, my students were going to do it more. If it wasn't, they were going to do it less. It was as simple as that.

Are there action steps you can take to highly motivate your students, so they will enjoy practicing and, consequently, practice more? Yes! In this book, I offer motivational techniques that I have found to be effective with my students. (All students' names have been changed.) I'll outline the *eight biggest roadblocks* to motivation and then follow up with an explanation of the *eight basic motivational styles* and how to activate them in the private studio or classroom. There will be plenty of ideas along the way about how to overcome hurdles and tailor your own teaching approach to match each student's personal motivational style.

There's even a quiz to help you and your students determine your top motivational styles. I originally encountered this quiz in a fabulous book called *The Motivation Breakthrough* by author and teacher Richard Lavoie. Thanks to his book, I learned these foundational keys to motivation, which I then applied to my own field of expertise. I'm grateful to him for endorsing my application of these principles to music teaching. These eight motivators have also become an essential part of the String Sprouts curriculum, a program I authored to reach children in underserved areas, which is now being offered to thousands of young musicians by the Omaha Conservatory of Music across the state of Nebraska and beyond. I've included more information about String Sprouts in the appendix of this book.

Wouldn't it be a dream to have every student who walks through your door end up highly motivated to practice? Notice I said, "*end* up highly motivated," not "*show* up highly motivated."

Why is that? It is a teacher's responsibility to connect with students and motivate them. Before this is possible, we have to know what does and does not motivate each student. We need to vary our approaches to motivation in order to reach every student.

If you are reading this book, I'm guessing you understand the importance of your students' motivation levels and are interested in adding new ways to motivate. After trying suggestions from this book, the best that could happen is higher motivation to practice from your students. The worst thing that could happen is that you'll maintain the status quo. What have you got to lose?

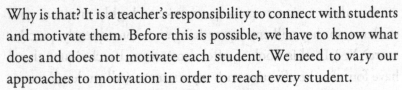

Chapter 1

MOTIVATION IS CONTINUAL

We are *always* motivated. Understanding this concept changes everything. Motivation is always present and is always focused on something. We tend to say someone is unmotivated to do something when, in reality, that person is simply motivated to do something else. In the music studio, "lack of motivation" means that a student's focus has shifted to something other than mastering their instrument. Factors that shift a student's motivation may be something a teacher cannot control, such as chronic stress or living in poverty. In other cases, particularly with things like poor teaching or a fixed mindset in learning, the motivational factors can be addressed by the teacher.

There's no doubt that every teacher would be thrilled if *every* student were totally motivated to practice and master their instrument all the time. This productive state of motivation nirvana would bring a steady stream of well-prepared young musicians to the studio for lessons each day.

However, more commonly than not, we have a mix of motivation levels, with some students willing to do just about anything for a sticker on a chart, while others could care less. Even the very best student has an ebb and flow of enthusiasm for practice, which swings between super-motivated and not-extremely-pumped-up. This is normal. And let's face it—if we honestly assess our own motivation levels as teachers, each week often brings a varying amount of enthusiasm for teaching, too.

In many studios, there is a variety of ability levels, from beginners to intermediate to advanced players. No matter the playing level, there will always be a range of motivation levels and a mixture of motivational styles.

Let's start by identifying three types of students that a music teacher might encounter. Each of these three types of students can exhibit different levels of motivation. In fact, a student from any of these three areas can have varying levels of motivation at different times on their musical journey. In other words, their proficiency level does not necessarily always match their motivation level.

Type 1: Self-identifies as a musician, highly skilled; usually motivated to "make it" in the music arena, regardless of periods of less motivation

Type 2: Interested in learning an instrument, not highly
skilled yet; can be prone to periods of disinterest,
resulting in lack of practice

Type 3: Uninterested student, often only present because
their parents made them take lessons

Any of these three types of students can be motivated,
regardless of their playing level. I don't buy into the idea that
there are some students who are just "good" (that is, hard-working
and motivated to practice) and others who are "bad" (that is,
uninterested and unmotivated to practice). Every student must be
developed into a "good" student by their teacher. Good students
are created, not born!

As my teacher John Kendall used to say, "Create the 'NO-
FAIL' environment!" By this, he did not mean that failure isn't
acceptable—often, a failed attempt in a practice session or lesson
is the very thing that's needed to actually learn. Mr. Kendall's
statement is focused on the teacher, not the student, and the
emphasis is on the word "create." In other words, the teacher has
a responsibility to continuously assess whether the environment
is working for the student's best learning. Is it so conducive to
learning that success will be the ultimate result? If not, make
changes, so the student can stay motivated and achieve their goals.

If we don't get to write off our unmotivated students, what
are we to do with them? We know there is potential for an
unmotivated student to become highly motivated, but how can

this be accomplished? The philosophy of Dr. Shinichi Suzuki declares, "Every child can learn." A teacher who truly believes this concept accepts the responsibility of taking a child from wherever they happen to be at that moment in their musical journey and building upon their experience to further their progress. I would propose that Dr. Suzuki's philosophy could be expanded to: "Every child can be motivated."

A student who is motivated to practice without any outside coercion is what we call intrinsically motivated. This means there's no external force that makes practicing a priority. This student just does it! Two neuroscientists, Edward Deci and Richard Ryan, developed a theory of self-determination. They asked the important question: What makes someone motivated to do something with no external forces at play? They came up with three elements that create intrinsic motivation:

1. Autonomy: Being able to do something on your own
2. Competence: Being able to do something well
3. Relatedness: Doing something in a community that values it

Said a different way: We like doing things we're good at, and it's even better when our community acknowledges how good we are.

My student Mark is a perfect example of how this works. Mark was pretty good, but he really didn't practice enough, and he also didn't practice very effectively when he did. Unbelievably, Mark won a concerto competition. He played very well on the day of the competition and won the opportunity to perform with an orchestra. His performance with the orchestra went well, with thunderous applause from his family and friends.

Guess who's practicing hours a day and attending every workshop and masterclass available? You guessed it...the now extremely motivated Mark! He won a competition (autonomy and competence) and then performed in front of his supportive community (relatedness). The intrinsic motivation has not worn off. He enters every competition now and is completely determined to win again. If you think about which of these three elements are present with your most motivated students, you'll probably see a pattern. I bet these three ingredients are at work!

Conversely, if you can identify what's missing in the environment for your least motivated students, you could work on developing an environment that would grow these characteristics. For example, organizing mini performances for a student in front of the people they love can boost relatedness. Make sure the student performs really easy pieces, though, to build up the competence factor. If they don't play well, it could have the opposite of the intended effect. Autonomy can be grown by allowing the student to pick a selection from a genre they really enjoy, whether it's fiddle, jazz, movie music, or show tunes. Once competence, autonomy, and relatedness are cultivated in the environment, motivation levels will grow exponentially.

As we begin to think about motivation within our studios, we need to ask a couple of important questions:

1. What types of students are in my studio? That is, do they self-identify as musicians, are they interested in learning but inconsistent in their engagement, or are they basically uninterested?

2. What level of motivation does each of my students have? For example, my student Jenny definitely self-identifies as a musician, but she is experiencing a lack of motivation right now. Jonathan is basically taking violin lessons because his mom enrolled him in lessons, and he has been relatively uninterested. However, he is really motivated right now by his current new piece.

3. Does my studio promote the three intrinsic motivators of autonomy, competence, and relatedness? Could one or more of these motivators be boosted in my studio?

While answering these questions, the issue of motivation is evaluated from both directions: the student's attitude and the learning environment provided by the teacher. Before continuing to read, I would suggest taking some time to write down your assessment of each student's current level of engagement. This will give you a record of where you started with each one. As you try different techniques with various students, you can keep track of what you've tried and how well it worked.

You can also make a list of ways you promote the three intrinsic motivators in your studio. If you notice that one of the intrinsic motivators has less emphasis than another, you can watch for suggestions that bolster this particular motivator to try in your studio.

Chapter 2

THE EIGHT ROADBLOCKS TO MOTIVATION

A good place to start on the road to motivating students is understanding their reasons for lack of motivation and then attempting to eliminate these roadblocks. If the deterrents can be removed, the road to motivation is much smoother, and any new motivational tools you try with your students will be that much more effective. A teaching zone that doesn't have any major de-motivators is likely a more productive place to hang out, anyway.

I discovered these eight roadblocks to motivation in a book called *The Motivated Brain* by Gayle Gregory and Martha Kaufeldt. It's an excellent and comprehensive read that highlights much of the research available on the topic of motivation. Whenever I'm reading about motivation, I always view the information from the angle of application to practicing and learning an instrument. When I became aware of these de-motivating roadblocks, I immediately started watching for these hindrances with students who were less than gung-ho about practice. In almost every case, one or more of the eight stumbling blocks was present.

Roadblock #1: Mediocre Teaching

I know...ouch! I decided to start with this one because it has the most hope of being eliminated. It's the one that teachers can control. I'm fully responsible for my level of competence as a teacher. Once I've taken responsibility for my own competence, I can begin to constructively work on areas in my teaching that can be improved.

We've all seen movies like *Mr. Holland's Opus* or *Music of the Heart*, about great teachers who—against all odds and obstacles—were able to reach their students wherever they happened to be. There are also those inspiring movies like *Freedom Writers* or *Dead Poets Society*, in which a teacher changes lives and motivates students to reach their potential. These teachers tapped into various motivational styles that helped students unleash their creativity or simply do something they didn't think they could do. The teachers often had to try more than one approach, but they kept trying until they were able to connect with the student on their level.

It's important to note that if a student is not motivated, it's never entirely the student's fault. We've all heard stories from teachers about how some of their students begrudgingly march in and out of their studios each week, completely uninspired. They are serving a sentence, decreed by a judge (their parent) and executed by the jailer (their teacher). We've also heard stories about the completely uninterested student who switches studios and becomes incredibly motivated. Somehow, the new teacher was able to find something that worked for this student and got them excited about learning.

Do I think it's possible to reach every single student all the time? Nope. But if it's not working, why continue to do the same thing week after week? Isn't that the definition of insanity—doing the same thing over and over, but expecting a different result?

Novelty is something that really gets our attention as human beings. We are designed to pay attention to what's different or new. An animal in the wild will first ensure its safety before curiously exploring the world around it. (More on this in Chapter 3: The Three Levels of Motivation.) We are the same—our attention will always evaluate what's new in our surroundings to determine whether it might be dangerous. We are built for survival first and then, once we are sure of our safety, we explore the new curiosities around us. The things we already know about in our environment are often dismissed as uninteresting. If you are not engaging, your students will not be engaged. On the other hand, if students don't know exactly what to expect when they enter your studio, they will be on their toes.

I know a conductor who uses the idea of novelty and unexpected behaviors with abundance. The results he gets with his youth orchestras are staggering, and it's not because the teaching is so much better than other youth conductors—it's simply because the students are paying attention. They are motivated to stay alert because they don't know what's going to happen next. This presents an element of perceived danger or curiosity.

How do we, as seasoned music teachers, combat mediocre teaching or apathetic teaching? How do we avoid getting into a rut with our teaching techniques or becoming a bit stale from overusing a teaching tool? We do it by embracing the concept of novelty, for our students and for ourselves. We need new things as much as our students do to keep our minds active and our studio culture interesting for everyone. Trying something new helps the teacher as well as the student!

If you are thinking to yourself, "I'm out of new ideas," here's a way to prime the pump. Think of a concept you teach frequently, perhaps a certain bow stroke. Brainstorm 10 analogies you could use to describe it. For example, the staccato bow stroke could be described as:

- A bouncing ball
- A row of bricks placed with spaces between
- A chicken pecking
- Like the sound of clapping

And so on! If you are truly struggling for new ideas, the internet is loaded with them. However, it's a fun and useful exercise to regularly challenge ourselves to think about something routine in a fresh way. Practicing creativity, just like practicing anything else, will strengthen the skill over time. Browse for ideas that others have had and use them as a jumping-off point for your own creative ideas.

I remember a lesson with a very advanced student where we were working on the opening of a concerto and its character. I had described the preferred tone quality many times, with specific technical suggestions, but she still wasn't quite able to hit the mark. Finally, I decided to ask her what she pictured when she played the opening phrase. She said it sounded like a group of riders on horseback. I suggested that maybe the riders were gnomes rather than full-bodied burly men. For some reason, this image struck the student as very funny. In the midst of chuckles, the student played the opening again. Wow, what a difference this mental picture made in the character of the musical idea! Because it was a brand new way of thinking about it, the student was able to grasp the concept quickly. To this day, she often recounts this lesson in particular, because it was so hilarious and so memorable for her.

There are many ways to inject novelty into the private studio, some in a musical way and some just for fun. Start a new practice contest. Use fresh vocabulary words in each lesson. Wear a series of silly hats, bow ties, or socks. Bottom line: Change it up! It doesn't really matter what you do differently as long as it's different. Novelty will boost attention and curiosity every time!

Besides these more extravagant uses of novelty, curiosity can be created by simply asking questions. Questions inherently arouse curiosity. The engagement we experience when we are curious nearly equals the level of engagement we experience when we are in sheer terror from something we perceive to be dangerous...but curiosity is a lot more fun than running for your life! Remember, an animal's attention is leveraged by two factors: survival and curiosity. Humans are no different.

Good students are always asking questions, either internally or out loud, about what they are learning. As teachers, we can foster this important skill by asking our students lots of leading questions during the teaching process. Rather than presenting our teaching points in lecture style or by simply "telling," try the Socratic method of drawing the information out through questioning. This teaches a curiosity-building skill valuable for lifelong learning.

Preschoolers ask around 100 questions per day, on average. By the time a child reaches middle school, the questions have almost stopped. It's a tragedy that our inborn nature of questioning diminishes as we grow older. When I realized this, I started paying attention to when I asked myself a question internally. I noticed that I actually did have lots of questions throughout the day, but since I was busy and had limited time, I would push these questions aside and squash my natural curiosity over and over. I decided to embark upon an experiment. I would require myself to look up the answer immediately to any question that popped into my head. I kept up this practice for a solid week. The most amazing outcome of the experiment was how much I learned that week. It was really fun and refreshing! It was also very interesting to note how much my curiosity increased throughout the week. My questioning nature was unleashed. Now, I have adopted the practice of looking up answers as much as possible. It's a way to nurture a learning attitude. In my case, curiosity didn't kill the cat, it woke it up!

I think it's important to touch on the idea of motivating through fear. Some teachers motivate by scaring students, deriding them, and making them feel very bad about their inabilities. Honestly, these tactics often do work—for a while. However, this approach violates the Law of Effect. Fear can create progress only in the short term. Since the participants in these situations are not experiencing pleasure, they will likely not clamor to continue if given the opportunity to quit.

The reaction to fear tactics depends on the student. When fear tactics are used with Type 1 students (those who self-identify as musicians), it has a minimal effect. The students aren't having a pleasant experience, but they are so committed to their instruments that they endure. With Type 2 or 3 students, fear can produce discouragement and widespread attrition. I consider this to be a mediocre teaching technique not only because it is limited in its effectiveness, but also because it allows the teacher to forego being creative in finding motivation tools for each individual student. A positive, loving approach to teaching will always yield a better and bigger result in the long run—no matter the type of student!

Roadblock #2:
Fixed Mindset Versus Growth Mindset

Fixed mindset means you believe you have a certain level of ability which is innate (sometimes called "talent") and that this level of ability doesn't change, even if you work really hard at something. Fixed mindset believes that hard work will never push a person past whatever talent quota they've been given.

The opposite of a fixed mindset is a growth mindset. A growth mindset means you believe that hard work is rewarded with progress. Increased effort and consistent discipline will produce results! The sky's the limit in terms of what can be achieved with this philosophy.

What's really interesting is the insidious nature of the fixed mindset thought process. Even if you proclaim to espouse a growth mindset, it's easy to have snippets of fixed mindset sneaking around, creating barriers to motivation.

I have a 10-year-old student who is playing the major concertos. She is considered "one of the best" in my studio. After a studio recital where she played brilliantly, I overheard another student of mine say, "I could never play like that; she's so talented." It was a golden opportunity for me to flip the switch from fixed to growth mindset, so I stepped up to the plate. I asked, "How much do you think she practices every day?" After I revealed that she puts in no less than two hours a day, I then asked, "How much do you practice every day?" Needless to say, it was far less than two hours.

The student suddenly realized that she has total control over how well she plays. Now, if someone had asked this student, prior to this conversation, whether she thought her effort mattered, she would have given a resounding, "Yes!" However, the fact that she attributed another student's success to straight-up inborn talent with little regard for the student's dedicated practice schedule shows that there was still some fixed mindset lurking in the shadows.

When combatting the motivation killer of fixed mindset, keep an eye out for comparisons, but don't avoid them. Comparisons can be detrimental or useful. When people compare themselves to someone else, they often aren't thinking about what their own effort can achieve but rather about what they are lacking. However, comparisons can be used to fuel a growth mindset if the analysis of what is lacking turns out to be something tangible.

A teacher can step into this situation and make sure the student thinks about the situation in a constructive way. For example, my accomplished student was practicing two hours a day. Extensive practice time can be emulated, so a comparison can promote a growth mindset. If the student making the comparison concludes that the other student's success is linked to effort instead of inborn talent, a switch to growth mindset can occur.

Another way to build a growth mindset is articulating expectations out loud. Examples of statements which will cultivate the right attitude are: "I can already tell you really understand this concept. With some dedicated practice time, you will be doing it exceptionally well by your next lesson," or "Wow, you've got the right attitude and understanding about this concept. I can't wait to see it in action at your next lesson!" Statements like these set a vision for the student's future and let them know you think they can do it.

Referencing past success builds up the student's confidence, too. This tool helps illuminate progress and remind students how much progress they've made. Make statements like: "I remember when passagework used to be such a challenge for you. Do you remember when you first applied this practice method and had amazing results? Let's do it again on this tricky spot," or "Think about a time you worked on a passage similar to this one successfully. What did you do to master it?" If a student is stuck on something in the present, you can work together to reference past triumphs and envision a successful future. This focuses on the growth mindset and helps make the attitude adjustment the student needs to do the work.

It's easy to compliment the achievements of students. However, I would encourage teachers to compliment the process and work that went into the achievement rather than the achievement itself. If I say, "I'm so proud that you won first place in this competition," I am risking the chance that this student stops focusing on growth and starts getting really "into their head" about always winning. A better approach would be, "You worked in such a disciplined way for so many weeks before the competition. I hope you can see how your dedication resulted in a great outcome."

Roadblock #3: Chronic Stress

It's no surprise that humans don't function as well when they are under stress. Stress has a way of blocking our creativity and causing problems with even our ability to think clearly. I think many adults are unaware of how stressed out kids are these days. Even if we do recognize rising stress levels, it's likely we've underestimated their severity.

A common cause of stress for students is overscheduling. A schedule that is way too busy is almost an epidemic with even the youngest of students. For example, I have a student who is in the third grade. I was hoping to move her lesson ahead by 15 minutes, but I quickly found out she was coming straight from another activity. Her lesson happened to be right before her group class experience at the Conservatory. (That makes three activities in a row, if you're counting: after-school activity, violin lesson, orchestra.) I asked if maybe I could move her lesson to after her orchestra class. Guess what? Not possible, since she had a mere 15 minutes to drive from the Conservatory to her final evening activity. Take a moment to imagine this child's day. After a full day of schooling, she went to four activities before returning home for the evening. No eating time, one activity after another, ending at 8:15 p.m. The parent was likely stressed out, too, driving the child to all these activities, but it probably paled in comparison to what the child was experiencing.

Circling back to the Law of Effect, being stressed out is NOT pleasant. If the high number of activities is causing stress, these activities become associated with the unpleasantness of a rigorous schedule. The student may begin to avoid preparation for these activities (such as practicing for an upcoming lesson). Even more likely, if the student is really overscheduled, chances are they are also overwhelmed. Being overwhelmed can cause paralysis, which looks a lot like lack of motivation. This probably goes without saying, but having a very busy schedule can also cause practice time to be limited simply because there aren't enough minutes in the day.

In comparison, my students with the most simplified schedules are generally doing the best. They have time to work through their lesson assignments, so they feel more prepared, which cuts down on stress levels. Also, the ability to focus on one thing usually creates a higher level of competence. A higher level of competence will generate motivation. We enjoy doing activities in which we excel.

Stress can also be caused by critical attitudes in the student's environment. If a student's parents are very demanding and react strongly when their child makes mistakes, the student will generally be fairly strung out. Often, this can cause the student to become very self-critical, which makes it harder to create an environment for learning. I've had students who put enormous amounts of pressure on themselves. No amount of compliments or encouragement will get them into a zen space. With students who are very self-critical, a teacher first needs to work hard to change the student's and the parent's attitude about mistakes and learning.

According to Daniel Coyle in his book *The Talent Code,* the optimal learning zone is at the edge of our ability, where mistakes are inevitable. Once the student (and the parent!) accepts that mistakes are simply opportunities to learn, the teacher can move on to the challenge of increasing motivation. I do want to point out that sometimes the parent does not change their critical manner with a student, but I have seen students overcome this criticism once they understand that they have to make mistakes in order to progress.

Another student of mine joined my studio when she was about eight years old. She was perfectly set up, extremely musical, and dedicated to practice. In other words, she was experiencing a lot of success and quickly identified herself as a "violinist." We had been working together for about a year when her parents decided to get a divorce. It was a hostile divorce, and my student's stress level was off the charts. What was so shocking to me was the screeching halt in her progress during the most turbulent time in the divorce proceedings. Even though she was practicing the same amount and continued to strive for excellence, her progress slowed to a snail's pace.

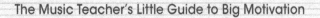

This period of struggle lasted for over a year. I was able to make some subtle changes to help her through this difficult period. Since she couldn't learn as much material, I started giving her smaller chunks with lots of different practice applications. Because I knew she was an organized, systematic person, it was somewhat therapeutic for her to complete her checklist of practice spots and achieve wonderful success on the smaller amount of repertoire required at each lesson. Over time, she picked up momentum again, but I was able to put her in a position to guarantee success during this period when her motivation level was affected by stress in her environment.

In many cases, there is no way for a teacher to remove a student's stress, but there are often ways to minimize its effect. If you sense a student is experiencing stress, try one or more of the following tools:

- Take time to talk with the student about how they are feeling and what challenges or successes they experienced throughout the week. Often, if they have the chance to vocalize their anxieties, they'll do better in the lesson and you will be able to give them better direction on how to improve.
- Offer the student the option to play a light-hearted piece without a huge amount of challenge. A break from rigorous technical work to focus on the fun of playing music can bring the same level of

refreshment and revitalization as taking a vacation from work. After relaxing with the "fun" piece, the student may feel less stressed and more ready to take on something more challenging.

- Back off on the amount you assign but provide lots of ways to fill the practice time with repetitions and interesting practice methods.

Roadblock #4: Expectation of Instant Gratification

Our world today is jam-packed with instant gratification—cell phone in our pockets, on-demand streaming videos, and all manner of conveniences "at the touch of a button." Learning an instrument *requires* the skill of delayed gratification, which is why the expectation of instant gratification can be a roadblock to motivation. The good news is that learning an instrument can also be a tool for *developing* delayed gratification, which has been shown to be a key indicator for a child's successful future. Parents who enroll their children in music lessons are taking a meaningful step toward developing the skill of delayed gratification in their children, bringing lifelong benefits.

In *The Talent Code*, Daniel Coyle says that you need 10,000 hours of practice to become an expert at something. To rack up that many hours of playing an instrument takes a good number of years, steady progress, and disciplined practice. Even the short-term goal of preparing a piece for a recital requires steady progress and disciplined practice. No matter how you look at it, music study is a long game that doesn't naturally provide a lot of instant gratification.

Some kids have the ability to stick to something even when the going gets tough and persevere through a challenge to gain the desired end result. Others tend to give up quickly if they can't do something immediately. For some students, it is very hard to see the big picture and to comprehend how consistent practice will eventually bring great results. Lack of motivation can be huge for these students. Teachers can focus on the little picture with these students by setting small, incremental goals.

When I break down goals into small, very achievable segments, I am simulating the feeling of instant gratification over and over, in rapid succession. As the student experiences small successes, the goals can become more robust and require longer runways. Over time, the student will realize the great success they have achieved by working hard to complete lots of small goals.

One way to approach this is to set a long-term goal (for example, a semester recital) and then work backwards with the student to schedule out the shorter goals. This allows a student who tends to gravitate toward immediate gratification to see the process needed to reach a longer goal. It also illustrates the milestones along the way that represent progress and success, which will feel gratifying.

Another effective approach can be using something the student really wants, such as candy or a trip to the studio treasure box. I often assign a rigorous practice plan or high number of daily repetitions for the week, which usually motivates practice. Be sure to make the prize valuable enough to warrant the work. If it's too much work or too difficult a goal, the student who needs immediate gratification simply won't do the work. Most students, regardless of their capacity for delayed gratification, don't have a well-formed concept of how much repetition is needed to achieve mastery. Recently, I've used weekly dot-to-dot puzzles with number totals of 300 and higher to increase the repetition levels of even my most advanced concerto-level students. They love it! After a while, an assignment to do 300 repetitions in a week seems like an easy task. When they return the following week with a completed dot-to-dot, they've earned a trip to the treasure chest, which has a collection of box candy and cool little prizes for all ages. The best part about these high repetition challenges is how accomplished and confident the student will be on the segment they have practiced thoroughly. I haven't had any students who didn't realize the value of these more long-term efforts.

Some students will be initially overwhelmed by an assignment to practice something 100 times every day. To address this, I will often ask the student to play the segment while I time it to determine how long it takes. We then proceed to do the appropriate math to figure out the total duration of practice needed to complete the repetitions each day. For example, if the segment takes two seconds to play, the student will need to play it for 200 seconds to get 100 repetitions completed. This amounts to a little over three minutes of practice. Three minutes is NOT very long at all. One of my families got a really awesome set of sand timers that have different amounts, from one minute to 10 minutes. They just flip over the sand timer and play the segment until the sand runs out. Their kids do a LOT of repetitions without any issues!

Each year, I like to set goals together with each of my students. This often involves planning the repertoire for the coming year to achieve the next level of graduation. We review the goals mid-year to evaluate progress, redirect efforts, or modify goals. At the beginning of the next year, I like to celebrate the goals that were achieved and set new ones. This process allows students to think more long term but also to understand the day-to-day work they do to achieve these goals.

Roadblock #5: Overuse of Technology

Technology can be a blessing and a curse for a young musician. Video games can easily suck away valuable hours of potential practice time. At the same time, technology offers young musicians unlimited access to great performances, masterclasses, and interviews with top artists to enrich their study of a piece. Such practice tools were not available at all only one generation ago. On the other hand, getting too accustomed to having all this information at our fingertips all the time brings us back to Roadblock #4—the expectation of instant gratification. It's a profound juxtaposition to think about the fast-paced, technology-driven world and the slow-paced, face-to-face experience of taking a music lesson. A music lesson is fast becoming one of the few remaining activities where learning is passed down from master teacher to student through extended periods of time. The incremental transfer of skills and knowledge must occur during one-on-one sessions over a number of years. We should not underestimate the incredible impact that these face-to-face, multi-year music lessons have on a child's development, particularly when compared to elements of other common learning environments, such as class settings with a different teacher each year and limited time for individual attention.

I do think music teachers can draw upon the motivational elements in video games to boost interest and engagement for students. Video games build in rewards and punishments in a safe environment. Players can fail miserably and go right back into the fray for another chance at victory. Video games also provide competition and achievement. Leveling up, gaining extra lives, and earning rewards all foster a sense of accomplishment. There's just enough tragedy and success to make players want to try again.

These strong motivators can be applied to music study. There are ways to create the experience of "leveling up" during sight-reading exercises or technical etudes. If you make it to the end of a line, you go to Level 2 and regain all your lives. If you make more than three mistakes in a line, you lose all your lives and start over.

A certain number of allowed "mess-ups" really helps create an environment where a mistake is just an opportunity. Developing a practice routine that resembles the mechanics of a video game can be revolutionary for a student who is not that interested in practicing but really loves the competitive and data-driven aspects of video games. Competitive practice games that mirror video games make practicing fun by pushing the student to try and beat "the big boss" (also known as the tricky passage in their piece).

Instead of framing the use of electronic devices as the opposite of musical training, you can incorporate technological tools to enhance the study of a piece. I always assign listening as part of daily practice. Students are asked to watch a variety of performances and tell me what they have observed. Why did they enjoy one performance more than another? These kinds of valuations encourage students to listen in depth and use technology resources in a relevant way.

I've also used elaborate metronomes and tuning apps. These can make practicing very entertaining. Students who are gadget-happy or data-driven like experimenting with these tools to enhance their practice sessions and track their progress. I once used a tuning app called Tonal Energy for a studio-wide competition. Each week, students would play their scales and try to improve their percentage of in-tune notes. They were competing with themselves to improve intonation, but also with other peers at the same level. I would post a leaderboard each week, so students would see whose percentage of in-tune notes was the highest. The end results were huge improvements in intonation over the course of the semester. My students still use this app regularly for intonation practice.

Roadblock #6: Social Isolation

There are many reasons that a student can feel isolated. The constant contact to the world allowed by cell phones and social media often brings a false sense of relationship and connection. Some other common causes of social isolation are language barriers, frequent geographical moves, issues surrounding sexual orientation, bullying, and sometimes just plain not fitting in due to lack of social skills (often a difficulty for kids who are on the autism spectrum). Since most of the work required to learn an instrument happens at home, during the time between weekly lessons, the daily home environment of the student dramatically impacts their ability to learn. Put more simply, they may not be able to prioritize their progress. They may be emotionally fatigued by situations in their school or home. It's much harder to learn when emotional resources are funneled towards self-preservation or managing difficult relationships.

This is where the long-term relationship between a student and their private music teacher can make a huge difference for the student in combatting social isolation issues. The music teacher is a very important long-term adult figure who can help the student navigate a lonely or treacherous social landscape. It's important to spend a little bit of time at the beginning of each lesson checking in with the student. How was their week? Or day? Were they able to practice as much as they had planned? If not, what were their biggest barriers? In particular, students who experience an emotional outlet through their music-making anticipate their lesson time as a safe haven and place for deep connection that they may be missing in other parts of their life.

If I suspect there might be issues with social isolation, I will encourage involvement with as many studio activities as possible. Any chance to have studio mates interact can lead the way to orchestrating friendships with like-minded peers. For students who have self-identified as musicians, the opportunity to connect with others is an absolute lifeline. I had a student who was a bit of a loner but worked very hard to join my premiere touring ensemble. After participating in her first tour, she declared, "I love this group! I've found my people!"

Roadblock #7: Lack of Real-World Application

One of my sons had difficulty at school because he felt like many of the assignments were busywork. To some degree, he wasn't wrong! For some students, if they can't figure out the benefit of what they are doing, they are generally much less motivated. As music teachers, we should try to give the student the "why" of an assignment. It can generate enthusiasm for the goal if they understand how and why it will help them. Inquisitive students will often ask why you want them to do something, which shouldn't be viewed as obstinate. An answer that includes a real-world application will ignite motivation in most cases.

I also strive to give meaningful assignments that aren't just busywork. My mentor John Kendall used to say, "We use our pieces to build our technique." If we assign a piece from the student's past repertoire, it's most effective when it directly relates to a technical challenge or skill the student is trying to learn at the moment. Review for the sake of review is still useful, but targeted review with relevance to current challenges provides twice the effectiveness: reviewing for refinement of older skills to develop true mastery and reviewing to provide repetition of a needed skill for a newer piece. This allows the student to focus on what they are trying to improve while playing music that is familiar.

Sometimes lack of motivation is related to lack of relevance to current culture. One of my friends once appropriately titled her music history class "The Music of Dead, White Guys." I think learning tunes outside the classical Western European master-works can be really fun and can also provide ample opportunity to teach universal technical challenges for any instrument. Case in point: Our beginning orchestra's favorite piece this year was "All About That Bass." Needless to say, they were very motivated to practice this tune and learned some great syncopated rhythms with interesting finger patterns in the process.

I'm always very willing to use contemporary tunes, especially when a student asks to learn something in a particular genre. If they really like a piece of music, they'll be much more motivated to practice.

Probably the most obvious real-world application is an upcoming performance. It's very motivating for students to share the music they've learned in performance. It doesn't have to be a formal recital or concert. Visiting a retirement home, playing at a farmer's market, or presenting a home concert provides an end goal and motivating reason to practice.

Roadblock #8: Living in Impoverished Conditions

Many of us can't relate to a daily life fraught with worry about where the next meal might be coming from or where you will sleep that night. The major concerns (food, water, rest, and warmth) are of the highest importance in psychologist Abraham Maslow's hierarchy of needs, and they're followed directly by safety and security. When basic needs aren't being met, it's not likely that practicing an instrument will be prioritized.

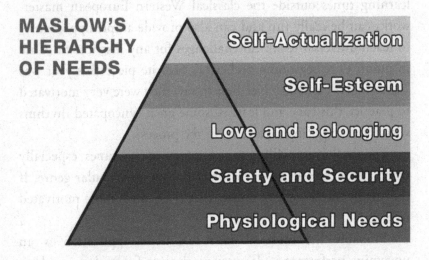

MASLOW'S HIERARCHY OF NEEDS

Self-Actualization
Self-Esteem
Love and Belonging
Safety and Security
Physiological Needs

The next step up in Maslow's pyramid involves family, friends, and relationships—the need to belong. Relationships

within a family can be strained when there is lack of money, job security, or even transportation.

Each of the stresses at the bottom of Maslow's hierarchy of needs decreases motivation for the items at the top of the pyramid: self-esteem and self-actualization. A student will be highly motivated to get food, sleep, and attention over the self-actualizing activity of mastering a new and challenging skill on their instrument.

The fact that a student lives in impoverished conditions is completely out of a teacher's control. However, we do have control over how we react to the student's lack of motivation in these circumstances. Often, the time spent in their lessons gives the student a brief reprieve from the outside world and the pressures it holds. I try to connect with the student at each lesson and give them a safe place to express themselves through music and conversation.

My assignments in this situation build skills slowly but, more importantly, foster joy and fun for the student. I try to praise the student for every small step of progress. In dire living situations, the top of Maslow's pyramid (self-esteem) will invariably be neglected. The lesson becomes a place where self-actualization and self-esteem can be nurtured as much as possible, no matter how much effort the student can give.

Chapter 3

THE THREE LEVELS OF MOTIVATION

We are always motivated, from the moment we awake until we lay down for a night of sleep. Our brains are constantly seeking something—it might be food, pleasure, relationships. This action of seeking is what we call motivation. How we manage our motivation shows in the results we produce.

There are three levels of motivation. Any type of student (self-identified as a musician, interested but inconsistent, or uninterested) can drift between these three levels of motivation, depending on circumstances. This idea can generally be applied to any activity in our lives. We can have various levels of motivation, depending on the day and the activities we encounter. As music teachers, we are challenged to move our students from the lower levels of motivation to the higher ones. In fact, I would venture to say that this should be a primary goal for a music educator. I routinely evaluate each of my students to determine their level of motivation. This helps me to give them a lesson that best fits with their motivation level and, hopefully, moves them forward from one level of motivation to the next.

The First Level of Motivation

The first level of motivation is the most all-consuming for the teacher to navigate. Initially, every brain is seeking the answer to one of these two questions: "What do I need to survive?" or "What is this new shiny thing?"

Survival will always be the primary concern of any animal, including humans. If a student doesn't feel safe, they will be looking for a way to escape, even if it's just through daydreaming. Some home environments are not healthy, with perhaps abuse, lack of food, or simply lots of fighting. Conditions that threaten physical and emotional survival override any other forms of motivation created by novelty or curiosity.

Any kind of emotional stress, like divorce, death of a pet or loved one, or anxiety about school can slow learning to nearly a halt as the student's motivation turns toward safety and away from learning. I had a student who was naturally gifted, picked things up quickly, and had excellent posture, which allowed her technique to flourish. Quickly, she became the superstar of the class. However, when she was about 10 years old, one of her parents became very ill. She suddenly couldn't memorize pieces as quickly as she had in the past. She also had a lot of difficulty staying tuned in during the lesson itself.

She continued with me into high school, but her upward trajectory never really resumed. Luckily, violin was one of the stable factors in her life during this difficult period, so regardless of how she progressed, it was an extremely valuable part of her life.

If the majority of a person's emotional, safety, and survival needs are being met, the natural curiosity can then be piqued with questions. The act of questioning wakes up the brain and engages the questioner's problem-solving skills.

Curiosity is also stimulated by novelty. The first level of motivation can sometimes require a pretty rigorous "dog and pony" show from the teacher, meaning quite a bit of entertainment to keep the student's attention. Finding ways to introduce different genres, surprise practice challenges, fun teaching tools (dice, spinners, etc.) and being slightly unpredictable in a fun way are good ideas to keep it fresh every lesson.

Finally, the lesson material has to be the most exciting and the most important thing happening. No amount of pontificating, trying to go deep, or long dialogue will keep the attention of a student in the first motivation mode. I have a delightful new student who is five years old. He is incredibly curious—in fact, just about everything seems like the most exciting thing he's seen or heard. My job is to keep the lesson moving at a fast pace and keep the directions short and clear. He is easy to teach, but if I were slow-paced and sluggish about directions, you can bet he wouldn't be easy.

Many teachers I know only keep students in their studio if they move into motivation stage two fairly quickly. The first level of motivation is definitely challenging, but it's also very rewarding. It's in this stage that the student learns to love music and their instrument!

The Second Level of Motivation

The second level of motivation is produced by what the seeker wants, not necessarily what they need. Over time, every person recognizes patterns of cause and effect. While the first level of motivation is mostly focused on avoiding pain, the second level of motivation is often inspired by the anticipation of pleasure or reward. If the music student has success with one mode of practice, which consequently produces a rewarding outcome, the student may begin to associate practicing with a positive result.

In order to set up the possibility for this positive connection between practice and reward to occur, a teacher needs to create successful routines for the student. Once a repeated occurrence of reward is established related to successful practice, the student's intrinsic motivation will be activated.

The student who implements excellent practice methods often feels much more prepared for a recital and has a far higher chance of giving a successful performance. A teacher should try to give students a long runway to their goal and provide many successful moments along the way to reinforce good habits and boost motivation. The second level of motivation is about building an arsenal of practice tools that produce great results. As these good results happen repetitively, motivation will continue to increase.

It's very important in this secondary stage to highlight connections between pieces for the student. The teacher can use phrases such as: "Where have we seen this kind of musical figure before?" or "Remember when you practiced the passagework in your concerto with this practice method? Is there anywhere in this piece that the method might also work?" If the teacher helps the student begin to make their own correlations, the student will eventually be able to learn, study, and interpret pieces autonomously. It's a great success when a student can extrapolate principles and understand how concepts in one piece can be applied to similar material in another piece. This skill is an essential component for a student to move into the third level of motivation.

A student can reside in the second level of motivation for a really long time—in fact, some students never graduate to the third level. Since the second phase can cover years of music study, stories of other musicians' successes can be very motivating. It builds up confidence and an attitude of success when a student relates their own experience to the experience of a great musician who has come through similar circumstances.

In the same way, it is valuable to share the success stories of one student with the other students in your studio. Sometimes it can even dispel some myths about why that student is so successful. Recalling the importance of the growth mindset: Are students thinking their abilities are fixed, or do they think hard work can produce better results? It demystifies the amazing performances of superstar students. Superstars work hard to produce that level of mastery. And guess what? The ability to put in the time is available to everyone.

A growth mindset needs to be cultivated constantly with young musicians. If a student thinks they are born with a finite amount of talent, what difference does it make how much they practice? This complicates efforts to create the relationship between good practice habits and the good feelings that come from this success, and this relationship is needed for the second level of motivation.

As a young musician, I sometimes bemoaned my fate in an audition for seat placement or some other competitive situation. My mom would always say, "It appears that you and _____ [insert name of competitor] are at about the same playing level. Your job is to practice so much that when the next competition comes around, you will have improved so much that there is no comparison." Essentially, the sage advice my mom was giving me was that working hard produces results and was directly related to my level of success.

Every teacher should be prepared to traverse back and forth between the motivation levels as they work with each student on their musical journey. Before the student graduates to the third level of motivation, the teacher may need to fall back on techniques they used in the first level of motivation related to novelty and surprise. If a secondary-level student's motivation wanes, a teacher can introduce a new piece, a new genre of music, a new practice chart, or even a new group activity where other students learn repertoire together. The combination of something new plus a good understanding of how practice will produce a good outcome can be a recipe for major success!

The Third Level of Motivation

Once students reach the third level of motivation, the teacher's role can change to pure teaching without a lot of attention to keeping the student engaged. Motivation is now intrinsic. These students don't need external help to stay motivated; they are truly motivated by the act of learning and playing music. They think creatively about how to play their assigned repertoire by considering phrasing and studying the details of their pieces.

A student in the third level of motivation notices patterns from their past experiences. They use these patterns to solve problems in a new piece without the help of the teacher. For example, when they understand that a gavotte almost always starts with two pick-up notes, the second of which should have a lift before the first downbeat, they can use this knowledge to interpret the pick-up notes in future gavottes they learn.

Students at this level will often request help from the teacher on very specific needs. They are able to understand their music-making from a broader perspective. A performance in which they have a few trouble spots is not generally devastating to their overall confidence and self-efficacy related to playing their instrument.

At the third level, a teacher can guide the student through the process of solving the musical problems they find in their new repertoire by reminding them to think about past solutions to similar problems. (This contrasts with the strategy in the second level, when the teacher may need to identify the connections for the student.) If the teacher continuously guides the student to make connections between the current challenge and effective solutions they've utilized for similar problems, the student will become more skilled at making these connections without help.

Just as a student in the second level can regress to the first motivation level, my students in the third level have sometimes briefly slipped back into the second level of motivation. There are several common reasons for this type of setback, including burnout from excessive high-stress musical activities like competitions or auditions, frustration and discouragement from a piece that's too challenging, or fatigue from a complicated and overly busy schedule. A solution for all three of these problems can be assigning a short, accessible piece. Students have fun learning a piece quickly. It can provide a much-needed break from the stress of performing competition repertoire, a short distraction from the technical challenge that's causing discouragement, or an achievable goal for times when a busy schedule doesn't allow enough time to master harder repertoire.

To illustrate how a single student can flow between types and levels of motivation, I'll tell you about one student who I started at the age of five. Patrick was not particularly excited to start playing violin. His brother had been studying with me for the last four years, so there was literally no novelty about what the experience would be like for him. In fact, his mother had told him that when he was five he would start learning the violin and do all the things his brother did. When he began, I would have categorized him as a Type 2 student, meaning he was interested in playing but not consistent or very skilled. His motivation was definitely at the first level. I worked very hard to keep him engaged with incentive charts and achievable goals so he would build up lots of positive feelings about his practice and playing ability.

It didn't take very long for Patrick to move into the second level of motivation. He progressed quickly because he did regular review, listened to his recordings a lot, and was quite an expert at making connections between pieces. He would easily see patterns in arpeggios and scales that appeared in a new piece and report all the pieces he'd already played that had the same arpeggio or scale passage. When we got to a certain piece in the repertoire that he didn't like very much, he slipped back into the first level of motivation quickly. I had to come up with lots of ways to help him get through the piece with the skills he needed. I introduced a fun fiddle tune to work on simultaneously, which was a huge help. Once we polished the piece that he didn't enjoy all that much, we moved on and he popped back into the second motivation level.

Somewhere around sixth grade, Patrick knew he was quite good at the violin. He wanted to play at school for his classmates in all the talent shows, and he volunteered for any solo opportunities. At this point, Patrick was a Type 1 student, self-identifying as a violinist. However, he moved in and out of the second and third levels of motivation until he reached high school. At this point, he had chosen violin as a future career. His motivation level was at the third level almost all the time. I say "almost" because everyone's motivation wanes from time to time in everything we do, but Patrick's commitment to the instrument as a Type 1 student was unwavering.

It's important to remember that any type of student, at any level of proficiency, can be in any level of motivation. Someone once asked me if I had ever encountered a beginning or intermediate level student who was a Type 1 student (self-identifying as a musician) and also functioning at the third level of motivation. The answer is a resounding yes! I have a young student who declared herself a violinist at the ripe old age of eight years. If I bring up a technique that is similar to something she's encountered in an earlier piece, she will automatically apply all the practice methods and technical advice without any direction from me!

Chapter 4

THE EIGHT MOTIVATIONAL STYLES

first encountered these eight motivators when I attended a session at a Learning and the Brain conference presented by Richard Lavoie on his book *The Motivation Breakthrough*. It was truly one of the most motivational lectures I ever attended, and I highly recommend his book to anyone who teaches anything. I immediately knew these motivators could be applied to the private music lesson and would be important tools for reaching every child in a way that would speak to them personally.

These eight motivators originated as a result of research done by the Mattel Toy Company in the 1950s. In the hopes of boosting sales, the company was interested in finding out what motivated kids to want certain toys. The following motivation

quiz, which first appeared in *The Motivation Breakthrough,* will help you determine your own motivators, as well as those of your students.

Take time now to take the motivation quiz and add up your totals. Once you have totaled all eight lists, circle your top two or three highest scores. Have your students take the quiz, too (in the case of very young students, the parent can fill out the quiz for their child). After the quiz, read on for suggestions on how to motivate students who do not have the same motivators as you.

As a music teacher, it's really important to know what motivates me personally. It's highly likely that I will try to motivate my students using the methods that would get me fired up. However, if I'm aware that my students are motivated differently, I can add elements to my studio culture that appeal to everyone.

What's Your Motivation?

To find out ways to motivate your students (and yourself), take this quiz on what motivates you, which is inspired by Richard Lavoie's work with children and learning.

1	2	3	4	5
Not often		**Sometimes**		**Constantly**

#1

_____ Highly verbal
_____ Good sense of humor
_____ Self-confident
_____ Popular
_____ Dislikes being alone
_____ Enjoys group work and teamwork
_____ Peer-oriented
_____ Generally positive attitude
_____ Outgoing and friendly
_____ Stylish
_____ TOTAL

#2

_____ Masters new material rapidly
_____ Very productive
_____ Good memory
_____ Highly verbal
_____ Very curious
_____ Enjoys independent work
_____ Extensive vocabulary
_____ Large fund of background information
_____ Self-motivated
_____ Decisive
_____ TOTAL

#3

_____ Fears imperfection

_____ Highly sensitive to criticism, reprimands

_____ Often requests confirmation, reassurance

_____ Peer-oriented

_____ Judgmental

_____ Fashionable

_____ Needs praise

_____ Self-critical

_____ Generally compliant

_____ Enjoys the spotlight

_____ TOTAL

#4

_____ Has passionate interests

_____ Avid, independent reader

_____ Large fund of background information

_____ Strong memory

_____ Enjoys experiments

_____ Asks questions

_____ Gives unique, creative responses

_____ Enjoys problem solving

_____ Gossips

_____ Volunteers

_____ TOTAL

#5

_____ Has strong opinions
_____ Wants/likes responsibility
_____ Argumentative
_____ Questions authority
_____ Complains
_____ Very persuasive
_____ Quick temper
_____ Unique sense of style
_____ Outspoken
_____ Vindictive
_____ TOTAL

#6

_____ Enjoys being in charge
_____ Involved in power struggles
_____ Has leadership qualities
_____ Self-confident
_____ Courageous
_____ Decisive
_____ Straightforward
_____ Independent
_____ Bears grudges
_____ Competitive
_____ TOTAL

#7

_____ Optimistic

_____ Self-assured

_____ Industrious

_____ Goal-driven

_____ Efficient

_____ Highly competitive

_____ Vain, self-promoting

_____ Enjoys the spotlight

_____ Sensitive, easily disappointed

_____ Enjoys performing

_____ TOTAL

#8

_____ Seeks and displays group identity

_____ Sensitive to the needs of others

_____ Skilled motivator

_____ Fears rejection

_____ Seeks adult attention

_____ Admires role models

_____ Helpful

_____ Cooperative

_____ Sensitive to disapproval

_____ Volunteers often

_____ TOTAL

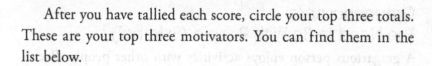

After you have tallied each score, circle your top three totals. These are your top three motivators. You can find them in the list below.

#1 Gregariousness: The need to be with others
#2 Autonomy: The need for independence
#3 Status: The need to feel important and valued
#4 Inquisitiveness: The need to know
#5 Assertive: The need to be heard
#6 Power: The need to be in control
#7 Achievement: The need to be recognized
#8 Affiliation: The need to be connected with something larger than yourself

Now that you know what your top motivators are, we'll explore each motivator and how to engage your music students effectively with each one. I've taken the eight motivators and grouped them into related pairs that can be addressed with similar strategies. Each pair has one motivator that is more internal (initiated by the individual) and one that is more external (relies more on outside influences).

Gregariousness:
The Need to Be With People (External)

A gregarious person enjoys activities with other people. Recall from Chapter 1 that one of the key components to staying motivated is doing an activity in a community that values it. This becomes even more important for a person with "gregariousness" as a primary motivator. I like to call this group "the party animals." There are so many excellent ways to motivate gregarious students.

Plan recitals with an afterglow. Having frequent recitals is important, since the gregarious student will have an opportunity to connect with their peers in the studio. For these students, what happens after the recital is as important as the recital itself. Make sure you plan a party, reception, or some kind of gathering following the performances. The social aspect of these fun celebrations can often be the reason a student sticks with their instrument during a rough patch in their practice careers.

Require group classes. Dr. Suzuki really got it right when he included group classes as part of the philosophy. Groups of students working together on the mastery of a piece is the gold standard for building community. It's truly doing something in an environment where it is valued. There's something extremely motivating about spending time with other students who are having a similar experience.

My touring ensemble, Frontier Strings, includes most of my students, as well as other top students from the community. In this group, we play many pieces in unison and some in parts. We incorporate Lindsey Stirling–style choreography and even do stunt fiddling. Many of the students are very close friends, and this group dominates their social and musical experience. It also incorporates varying ages and levels. This gives the older students the opportunity to mentor the younger ones, which plays into some of the other motivators, as well. Groups like this bolster the gregarious student's need for relationships and interaction as they develop their skills. Most of the students in this group would not dream of giving up their instrument, and they are highly motivated to learn new music and excel as an ensemble.

Encourage concert attendance. Concerts are perfect community events for a gregarious learner. The possibility of attending with friends adds exponential value to the experience. In many cases, concerts have pre-event talks or lecture opportunities. These pre-concert talks usually include tidbits about the personal lives of composers or "meet and greets" with the soloists. Learning more about the composers and performers provides an extra layer of connection, which enhances a gregarious student's enjoyment and presents additional pathways for deeper learning.

Encourage participation in youth orchestra. Playing in an orchestral ensemble is a must from the earliest age possible for this type of student. It's rewarding to play with others, in general, but for the gregarious student, the social network that develops within a youth orchestra is paramount. The orchestra provides access to "their people" and provides motivation to keep progressing with their peers.

Offer chamber music experiences. If playing in a youth orchestra is a great motivation, a chamber music experience is often like orchestra on steroids. The student not only plays their own part, which allows for a very personal expression of their musical voice, but the chamber music rehearsal is conversational, social, and highly cooperative—a gregarious student's dream!

Arrange non-musical gatherings. In my studio, we have massive cookie-decorating parties and frequent board-gaming sessions. As the students strengthen their non-musical bonds, the musical product is also strengthened, not to mention the support each student feels from their peers. In the competitive and sometimes cutthroat world of music, a supportive culture is one to be cherished.

Affiliation: The Need to Be a Part of Something Bigger Than Oneself (Internal)

Affiliation is the internal twin to the external gregariousness. A student who has affiliation as a primary motivator will need ways to show the pride they feel in being a part of a studio, school, or class. These students always want all the swag! If there's a t-shirt, hoodie, bag, or school sticker, they've got one, maybe several... they love uniforms or identifying objects that show who's a part of the group.

Belonging and contributing are paramount for students who are motivated by affiliation. These students become the spirit leaders of every group where they connect on a deep level. Affiliation students play a huge role in developing stronger community bonds between others in their circle. They also require a strong sense of community in order to really thrive and be motivated themselves.

There is a system of non-profit, public charter schools in the United States called the Knowledge is Power Program (KIPP). I read a book about a KIPP school in Chicago that accepted kids who were at high risk for dropping out of school. On the first day, they used something called a KIPP indicator to create cohesion within the student body. They would tell the group something like this: "You all are extremely special. You have been chosen specifically to be a part of this group. You are all destined for success and will attend college after you graduate." This group identity is reiterated over years of schooling. Of course, the students are extremely successful, and an extremely high percentage of graduates go on to attend college.

Jessica Davis, one of the superstar instructors at the Omaha Conservatory, works with students in a school focused on helping underserved students reach their potential. Every student at this school plays violin in the Conservatory's String Sprouts program. One year, she had a class that was struggling with the technical issues presented in the curriculum. She decided to use the KIPP indicators and tell the students they were her absolute best class for working on and perfecting these techniques. After months of work and constant reinforcement about how incredible they were at mastering these difficult skills, guess which class was excelling at this technique? This class had emerged as truly "the best."

I have used this technique often to strengthen and unify the purpose of a group. When I set them apart as a special group and vocalize a vision for their future, their motivation levels rise to meet the challenge of the vision that's been articulated for them. Particularly with students motivated by affiliation, their buy-in to this vision fuels motivation for the whole group. They can often assume the role of cheerleader for the group, which is a huge help in keeping everyone pumped up and pushing toward realization of the vision. This is just one of many ways to make affiliation a part of your studio or classroom.

Create studio clubs. Creating clubs within your studio is not hard. I posted two sheets of paper in my studio—one labeled "The Scale Club" and the other "The Arpeggio Dojo." After setting a few requirements for membership to each club, I offered opportunities for membership at each lesson. For example, an advanced violin student might need to play the entire arpeggio series from memory to be inducted into the club. Once they had done so, I would write their name on the "The Arpeggio Dojo" sheet. Requirements might vary, depending on the level of the student, but everyone would have an opportunity to be a member. Once they had achieved membership, additional stickers or checkmarks were added after their name when they had mastered another musical key skill. There were no meetings, dues, or other awards attached to these clubs, but kids worked hard to gain their membership.

Post a studio "Student Quote of the Week." Since every student enters the studio every week, you can create a sense of membership in an exclusive club by posting things students say during lessons, especially things you think are important for the rest of the studio to hear. For example, one of my students joyfully declared in her lesson, "I just love second position—it's so convenient!" Since second position is generally not the easiest position to learn, I thought this statement might be inspiring to someone struggling to learn the new position. This student was also admired as a great player by the other students in my studio, which added to the validity of the statement. Student quotes also create community by allowing other students to participate in a peer's lesson vicariously. It helps the students to remember they are part of something bigger than just attending their own individual lesson each week.

Create collaborative studio projects or awards. Each semester, I develop some kind of special challenge or award that every student is working on. Progress is tracked in some way in the studio. This is always really motivating to the affiliation kids, especially if there is a collective goal. One year, the prize was a cookie-decorating party. The challenge was to practice a certain number of hours collectively. I had calculated the amount of practice I expected from each student, added all the students' totals together, and then subtracted 15 percent, so the goal would be achievable but still rigorous. The progress each week was tracked on a giant thermometer, where I colored in the total amount practiced each week. As the temperature rose each week, the students felt like they needed to do their part, and they really enjoyed the group reward at the end of the process.

Provide t-shirts and swag. Anything that creates a studio identity will make the students feel like they are part of something bigger than themselves. Group identity can keep students engaged who are struggling individually. It can be a t-shirt, a sticker for their case, or just about anything that helps another member of the studio know that this other student is part of the same classroom. It can even be an inside joke or mascot. My husband teaches strings at the elementary level. One day, he mentioned something about the cello's C-peg and posture. One of the students misheard him and thought he said, "sea pig." A sea pig happens to be a real ocean creature, so my husband purchased a sea pig stuffed animal.

This stuffed sea pig has become the class mascot, and there are now special Sea Pig awards in the class. The sea pig has taken on the role of posture inspector, monitoring various posture points throughout the class. This unifying mascot brings a lot of fun and entertainment to the class. It's even more meaningful to this group of students because it was a student who brought the mascot to life.

Publish a studio newsletter to celebrate student success. It's fairly easy these days to create a web page for your studio. Any kind of studio newsletter brings the families together and celebrates the successes of students in a bigger way. Honoring students for their accomplishments can bolster other students' ambition. Student accolades also create an exclusive community and feed the status/achiever students (more on them later!)

In *The Talent Code,* Daniel Coyle mentions the idea of the role model or someone to look up to as an integral part of developing talent. As students learn about new opportunities, they can set future goals, and they've already watched their peers succeed. Running a four-minute mile was seemingly unachievable until one person broke through the barrier. Then, lots of people were able to do it. Once the first one of my students won the regional competition and moved on to compete at nationals, other students began to achieve the same success, year after year.

Do meaningful warm-ups as a group. My touring ensemble Frontier Strings has a couple of silly chants we do together to get warmed up. These chants are done in secret, which makes them even more special. Once you become a member of Frontier Strings, you are included in the warm-up chants. This idea of a secret warm-up or meeting time could be implemented prior to any studio activity, recital, outing, or community performance.

Make introductions. When students pass each other at back-to-back lessons, make sure to introduce them to each other. Sometimes I even share a little bit about what the students are working on. For example, "Hey Jasmine, this is Rachel. She's getting ready for a competition, so she's preparing four different pieces at the same time. Rachel, Jasmine is also working on preparing repertoire for an audition video for summer camps."

This is a simple thing, but it can go a long way toward building affiliation within a studio (and also motivating students to think about competitions and summer camps).

Assertiveness: The Need to Be Heard (External)

The students motivated by assertiveness want to have a voice and generally do not wait to be asked about their opinions. The assertive student may come across as argumentative, especially if their opinions are in opposition to what is happening around them at the time. However, when their ideas are acknowledged and even spark meaningful discussion, this can be significant motivation to these students. It's of high importance to a student motivated by assertiveness to know that their ideas have been heard, and there are many ways to make sure this happens in the classroom or studio.

Ask their opinion. The best way to motivate a student who is assertive is by authentically asking for their opinion. I know this may seem like a simple answer, but it's something that may not occur very often for this type of student. Teachers like to be right, respected, and considered the authority. It's easy to forget to offer the opportunity for assertive students to weigh in with their ideas. If there's a way for me to hear the student's opinion and use the follow-up discussion to motivate their creative thinking further, I'm going to do it. A good place to ask for opinions is on phrasing issues, since there is often more than one good way to phrase a passage. Playing two viable possibilities for the assertive student and then asking their opinion about which way they prefer is a fantastic way to get them excited about a piece. Even better is the follow-up question: "Why do you like this way better?"

Ask them to elaborate. Assertive students are generally very vocal. They will enter the studio and tell you exactly how they are feeling, why they are feeling that way, and what they think you should do about it. Here's what one of my most assertive students said to me at the beginning of a lesson before her upcoming college audition dates: "I've had a lot of trouble with memory spots in my unaccompanied Bach. I'm getting very worried that this isn't at the same level as my other rep, so I want to work for the first part of my lesson on memory practice suggestions. I'd like to touch on all my other repertoire, if possible, too, so hopefully it won't take the entire lesson."

When an assertive student makes a statement about something, I'll often have them elaborate on why they've voiced this opinion. As the teacher, you may be able to give them reasons beyond what they can articulate. This builds up their motivation, because they will have even more support for why they are doing what they are doing.

Lead them from problem to solution. When an assertive student expresses dissatisfaction or angst about something, it's important to ask them what they think would solve the problem or help in the situation. Sometimes, they are fully aware of how to fix it and just want to let you know they are struggling. However, if they do need help solving the problem, the assertive student often needs to talk it out. They can be prone to focusing on the problem, but moving them through the problem-solving process to land on possible solutions will be motivating.

After my assertive student told me about her problem memorizing the Bach, I asked her what things she had tried already. In the course of the conversation, I learned she had identified several short spots which were very similar and were causing her problems with memory. Since she had already identified the exact places where the problem occurred, I was able to add chord analysis to her knowledge base, which helped her understand how the small note differences were informing the harmonic structures of the piece.

In line with her assertive motivational style, later in the semester, she loudly contributed during a masterclass to a conversation about memorizing with the following statement: "Chord analysis and understanding the harmonic progression really helps solidify memory!"

Facilitate a discussion. Forums which allow for conversation about a musical topic, composer, technique, concert offering, or anything else are quite stimulating to this type of student. The voicing of their opinions is a primary source of contribution and adding value for them. At the Conservatory, we held a visioning session for teens. A great group of students gathered to express their ideas about what they'd like to see in the future and what made them excited about the Conservatory. We had to call an end to the meeting after over an hour of scintillating discussion.

You could really tell that a good number of these students were motivated by the opportunity to share their thoughts and assertively impact the future of the Conservatory's offerings.

Acknowledge that they've been heard. Undoubtedly, there will be times when things don't go exactly the way they were supposed to go...programs have misprints, difficult decisions go against the ideal, or outside competitive opportunities include some elements that aren't totally fair. Whatever the mishap, the assertive student will be quick to speak their mind about the situation. I respond in this way: "I hear what you're saying. Thanks for telling me your thoughts! We'll keep working on that." I don't actually have to do anything about the problem right at that moment. The best action is simply acknowledging that they've been heard!

Power: The Need to Be in Control (Internal)

While assertiveness is more externally manifested, the power motivator is more internal in nature. Students who are motivated by power tend to be natural leaders. They are motivated by being "large and in charge." A student with this primary motivation style can be a blessing or a curse in the classroom setting. Just like Spider-man found out, "With great power comes great responsibility." When a power student is operating with responsibility, it creates a wonderful leadership opportunity. On the flip side of the coin, a power student without a sense of responsibility can bring chaos and disruption to a class setting. There are several ways to nurture a student motivated by power.

Assign mentoring duties. A power student really enjoys being paired with a less-advanced student. These pairings can be as simple as assisting a newer or beginning student through the "ins and outs" of a recital, or it can be more in-depth, as a practice buddy or accountability partner.

Another important mentoring moment is actually as students cross paths between lessons. I mentioned earlier that I always make sure to introduce the student who is leaving their lesson to the student who is entering the studio. Besides creating a sense of family within the studio, a less-advanced student will witness how the older student acts as they finish or start their lesson. If the student is a power student and I know it, I will use this opportunity to motivate this student by pointing out leadership aspects of the power student's behavior.

For example, I have an advanced power student, Michael, who has a lesson right after Kyle, a student motivated by gregariousness. The gregarious student is excited to chat with the power student who is entering the lesson, so I'll interject something about the success of the power student to open the conversation. I might say something like, "Come on in, Michael. Kyle, Michael just finished every single scale in the Flesch Scale studies for the first time through the book. Michael, tell Kyle what you've improved on the most, since he's just at the beginning of his first trek through Flesch. What does he have to look forward to?" This kind of interaction builds up the power student's desire to lead, and it creates a nice exchange between the students, motivating the gregarious student.

Switch roles. There's nothing more fun for a power student than getting to be the teacher. Allowing students to assume the role of teacher also provides the teacher with the opportunity to demonstrate, in an exaggerated way, any problems the student might be having. These can be related to behavior or to posture and technique. If a power student keeps interrupting the lesson, be sure to interrupt like there's no tomorrow once the tables are turned! The only caveat is to be careful to keep this exercise light-hearted. The moment the activity begins to feel punitive or ridiculing, the teaching moment is gone.

Assign leadership roles. Any time you can give leadership tasks to a student motivated by power, you will develop not only a great helper but also the student's ability to lead through service. Suggested leadership tasks could be organizational, like overseeing the tuning of younger students at the beginning of a recital or group class or managing the details of the party following a recital. There are also opportunities for musical leadership. For a group performance, bring up a student leader and allow them to guide the class through a piece. This exercise provides the opportunity to teach good leadership skills, such as how to give a good cue and make eye contact with the members of your group. Students can also provide feedback on what they need to see in order to follow well, and the student leader can try to improve their direction to match the suggestions of the group.

Let students make decisions. When a power student gets to choose the order of their lesson, it immediately offers them a measure of control. As the teacher, you know what has to be achieved in a lesson, but the order in which it occurs is not always significant. If it is necessary to do the lesson in a certain order, you can still try to find a few ways to offer choices throughout the session.

Study musical leaders. It can be very useful to present music industry leaders as role models and then articulate what makes them good leaders. If you can generate a list of good leadership traits that are exhibited by key musicians, it's easy to make these traits desirable to aspiring students.

I often use Pablo Casals as an example, since there are written accounts of some of his habits. Casals was known for his supreme tone and phrasing. He practiced open strings regularly, sometimes for up to an hour a day. He would play complicated passages and entire pieces on open strings in order to really hear what his bow was doing. In this way, he was able to create a beautiful phrase shape before adding the fingering over the bow's handiwork.

Another example is Jascha Heifetz, who was known for his devilishly fast tempos. In an interview, Heifetz attributed his ability to play fast to regular practice of trills. There is an entire segment of the Kreutzer etudes dedicated to trill practice. I always tell my students this Heifetz story as they embark on this series of trill etudes to motivate them to practice their trills diligently. They might be able to play as fast as Heifetz if they do!

I once had a master's degree student who was notorious for getting tangled up in fast passagework and experiencing a great deal of trouble getting quick sections up to tempo. He decided to practice trills daily for one hour to improve his ability to play fast. After one semester of hourly practice on trills, he was notably more proficient at passagework and less likely to get tangled up on a tricky spot. He would never have been motivated to try this without first hearing this story about a leader in the industry who he highly respected. Sharing stories about great players who achieved excellence through practice and discipline is always motivating. Sometimes, it's easy to forget that these great players had to practice a lot, too.

Have discussions. It's always fulfilling to a person motivated by power to be treated as an equal. If a teacher can engage in meaningful discussions with students motivated by power, they will strengthen the bond between themselves and the student while at the same time motivating the student. Power students have lots of ideas about how to do things. In discussion, a teacher can shape an idea that needs tweaking, encourage the student to act upon on idea that warrants attention, and even discourage an idea that might not be the best pathway for success. If there is a difference of opinion, a teacher skilled in the motivational styles can lead the student to the right end point through questioning and persuasive stories. In general, getting into a fight doesn't result in motivation.

The student might begin to view the lesson as an experience that is not positive or is even a bit scary. If this unpleasant experience is repeated regularly, the Law of Effect will come into play, and the student will begin to shy away from the lesson.

Status: The Need to Feel Important and Valued (External)

Students with status as a primary motivator thrive on public affirmation of their accomplishments. Special titles, rewards, and awards are key tools to motivate this type of young musician. They are motivated to work hard for these accolades when they know how they will be publicly acknowledged for reaching the goal.

One trend in our society should be mentioned because it dramatically affects status students and their motivation. This trend is the participation trophy. Our culture has moved away from being competitive in a lot of scenarios. When every single student gets the same reward, no matter the level of their contribution, this will not motivate status students. In fact, they may decide that the activity is a total waste of time, so beware of overusing universal awards. Status students are better motivated by rewards that are keyed to actual contribution.

Post sticker charts. Each semester, I post a studio sticker chart. Students gain a weekly sticker for a stated goal at the beginning of the semester. These stickers have been associated with a wide range of goals. One semester, it focused on practicing each item listed in your practice journal five times per week (to make sure students weren't neglecting certain areas of practice and spending all their practice time on other areas). Another semester, I assigned a listening challenge for the weekly sticker. Sticker charts are usually public and are used to recognize the effort of all the students in a studio toward reaching certain landmarks or achieving established goals.

It becomes obvious which students are motivated by status and which are not, since the status students will make sure their sticker is added each week and will remind me if I forget! On the other hand, those who could care less about a sticker chart often won't even pick their sticker, allowing me to do it for them. As students get older, they are frequently less interested in the sticker chart, but I always tell them that they are mentors for the younger students. I'll let the older students know that the younger students are watching their progress—if there are a lot of stickers missing, these younger students have gone so far as to ask me about it! Usually, older students will go along with the sticker chart when they know how meaningful it is to the younger ones.

Create a studio challenge with rewards. One of the most successful studio challenges I have used involved tracking general and active listening. Students would keep track of all their listening minutes per week. The students were grouped with students at about the same age and level. Each week, I would post a leaderboard with the listener who had the most minutes for that week. At the end of the semester, there were rewards for the student who listened the most in each group, the group that listened the most overall, and the individual student who listened the most from all the groups. The combination of individual awards and group awards motivated status students as well as affiliation students.

I have had alumni status students, who have graduated and gone on to college, reminisce with me about a particular challenge that occurred during their time in my studio. They remembered it as lots of fun and very motivating!

Offer special awards. My ensemble Frontier Strings performs frequently in the Omaha area and also tours nationally each year. Since the group is known for their incredible stage presence and showmanship, we have established three areas of achievement (beyond playing the music well) that we want to recognize: good facial expressions, correct use of the bow (how much and where), and physical movement with the music. We have three stuffed animals that are awarded after every performance, each with its own meaning. The first is a stuffed unicorn, representing the most magical performance. This usually goes to the person with the strongest facial expressions and genuine enthusiasm for the performance. Our second award is a stuffed monkey. The monkey has evolved over time to include a wardrobe of a crocheted hat and sweater in winter and a bathing suit in summer. (All of these additions were completely generated by the kids themselves!) The monkey goes to the student who "went bananas" during the performance. This means they used a lot of physical energy in movement and use of their bow. Finally, there is a stuffed squirrel for the performer who "went nuts," which means having the best overall presentation of the three desired characteristics. The squirrel is awarded by the student who won the squirrel after the previous performance. This "peer to peer" award also creates feelings of affiliation, ownership, and responsibility for the group. These three awards are coveted, and the awards ceremony following each performance is highly anticipated!

Bestow special titles. It can be very motivating for a status student to fulfill a special role in class. You can choose a student to play the "A" drone during tuning time and designate them the Tuning Wizard. There can be an Exercise Guru who leads stretches before a rehearsal. Several of my students in the Frontier Strings are designated as Spirit Leaders. It's also important to call out students by name. Trying to say each student's name at least once during a class is another easy way to pump up the motivation level of status students. People like to hear their names. Add some kind of compliment, and you've really got a winner. "I love the way Johnny's bow is right on the bow path."

Provide progress reports. Each year, I set four technical or musical goals with each of my students. We also discuss areas where we hope to see improvement. When we review the progress from the preceding year in order to set new goals, there is always an opportunity to boost the motivation of the status student. If at all possible, make sure the parent is in the room as you review which goals have been achieved. When the student is acknowledged for their progress in front of their parent, the experience is even more meaningful. If you post a list of the students who achieved all four of their goals, this adds another layer of richness for the status students.

Promote great recital experiences. In general, a status student enjoys the appreciation of a crowd for their performance. However, it's key for a teacher to help the status student select a piece that can be well-prepared and is likely to produce a rewarding experience. I usually try not to select the most recent piece they've learned for my studio recital. A performance that goes well will feed the student's motivation. A poor performance can cause great damage to a student's motivation, regardless of their motivational style, but for a status student, it can be debilitating. I had a status student who decided to play a fairly new movement of a Mozart sonata. I encouraged her to use the music, as is typical of this type of chamber music, but she wanted to play it from memory. Against my better judgment, I allowed it. During the recital, she fell into the trap of not modulating back to the tonic key in the recapitulation, but rather moved to the dominant key used in the exposition. The mistake resulted in a complete stop. She had to find her place by looking at the pianist's score and then stumbled her way to the end. It was literally years before her confidence in her memory skills returned.

Provide extra performing opportunities. Since every student performs at a studio recital, it doesn't spark the highest level of motivation for a status student. These students are better motivated when they set up their own unique performances, like playing at an assisted living facility. Several of my families play regularly at the farmer's market or on busy street corners in Omaha's historic downtown area. For the students with high status motivation, this type of performance is exciting and compelling. One such student learned a showpiece in record time. He had attempted a portion of the piece prior to being completely ready but still scored a twenty-dollar bill from a passerby. He lovingly called that selection "his money piece."

Achievement: The Need to Produce Results and Be Recognized (Internal)

As a motivator, achievement is the internal complement of status. A person who is motivated by achievement will be driven by their desire to reach goals and will continue to work hard until they are recognized for their results. When they are recognized, it fuels them to push hard again for the next achievable outcome. Many of the same motivational tools that work with status students also work with achievement-driven musicians, but the motivation is more directly related to achieving a defined goal. With this subtle difference in mind, let's explore some ideas for motivating the achievement student.

Encourage participation in competitions. A competition provides an extremely clear end result and usually has very clearly outlined requirements (for example, one movement of a concerto, a twenty-minute program with two style periods represented, repertoire pre-selected by the competition sponsors). The achievement students will prepare with intensity and intention, while a student who is not motivated by achievement may place less importance on the competition itself. Competitions are a necessity for the achievement student but are not required for other types of students.

Outline goals clearly. The goals for this type of student should be very clearly outlined, and then it's really important to follow up. The achievement-based student will hold themselves very accountable to whatever the goals for the week may be, and they need to hear or see the affirmation of this achievement in the lesson. My achievement students will always remind me if we haven't put the weekly practice sticker on the chart. They could care less about other students seeing their sticker; they want the joy of seeing their practice rewarded by putting the sticker on the chart. It's the equivalent to marking something off of a list for those people who love to make lists and check things off.

This particular motivational style happens to be one of my primary motivators. This probably explains why I make up to 35 resolutions every New Year's Eve, which are related to seven areas of focus. At the end of each year, I evaluate all of my resolutions and give myself a percentage of achievement for the year. Over several decades, my percentages have risen dramatically, which is incredibly fulfilling to me. If I have an achievement student, I will help them set long-term goals similar to my resolutions tradition. Together, we create goals related to several different areas and

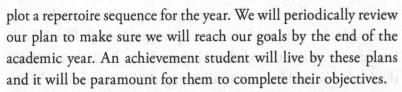

plot a repertoire sequence for the year. We will periodically review our plan to make sure we will reach our goals by the end of the academic year. An achievement student will live by these plans and it will be paramount for them to complete their objectives.

It can also be inspiring to the achievement student to use specific repertoire lists, such as the various levels of Royal Conservatory of Music requirements, Suzuki Book Graduations, or String Sprouts Sprouting Up Ceremonies. They can see all the levels and what's required right from the outset. They will be driven to complete all the levels and won't stop until they've achieved it.

Praise progress. It's important to compliment the tiny advancements a student makes from week to week. Honest praise for even the smallest accomplishments is meaningful to all students, but it is particularly important to achievement students. When an achievement student reaches a goal, it actually spurs them on to set a new goal and work toward it.

If a student isn't prepared for a lesson, some amount of browbeating might be justified. Usually, students are highly aware if they are not meeting standards or simply not playing all that well. However, achievement students are particularly notorious for self-criticism. The teacher has to balance the negative and the positive to keep the student motivated but also give them a more productive pathway to preparation.

Bestow special awards. I've mentioned special awards as a motivation for status students. For achievement students, special awards that allow them to compete against themselves are invaluable. My advanced students try to get through Flesch Scale Studies at least five times before they graduate. Each time through the book, they add a new challenging skill for each key. When they have played the required portions for each key, they get a giant box of Nerds at the studio recital and are dubbed a "Scale Nerd" for the semester. The other students are encouraged to continue working on their scales, especially when a high schooler gets the "Scale Nerd" award for their fifth time through Flesch. It makes this high level of achievement seem possible.

I have sometimes noticed a subtle watering down of a student's accomplishments when they are being honored in front of their peers. I assume this is an attempt to keep other students from feeling bad about themselves, but I find it counter-productive. I highly suggest making a huge deal out of the high level accomplishments of any student who does something extraordinary. It will only motivate the rest of the students to see what they can achieve next. Also, we shouldn't sacrifice what the achievement students need just because their peers might not be motivated by it.

Provide progress reports with checkpoints. As I mentioned earlier, it's extremely important with status students that their parents are present when progress reports are being reviewed. With achievement students, it's less important to have the parents present, but goals still need to be periodically reviewed. This allows the teacher to spur on the student if they are falling short of the goal in some way. It's pretty crushing to get to the end and not achieve an important goal, but sometimes a mid-court adjustment can really do the trick.

One of my achievement students was preparing a rigorous National Music Teachers Association program with the hopes of moving on to the regional competition. We set this program goal nearly eight months in advance so we would have time to periodically check in with our goals to see if they still made sense. About four months before the competition, it became very clear to both me and her that one of the pieces wasn't going to be ready. We knew the piece would cause a huge amount of stress and probably would not match the high level of preparedness already achieved on the other repertoire for the program. Because we had prepared our checkpoints so far in advance, we had time to switch out the piece with another equitable selection.

Another of my achievement students would enter every competition, prepare splendidly, and often play the best of all the competitors. Unfortunately, it never earned her a first-place win or even any acknowledgement. Be ready to coach achievement students through these disappointing times. If, for some reason, a clearly outlined goal is not achieved, take time to talk through why there was a shortfall and how it can be avoided in the future. Be sure to highlight any aspects that went well. Also, teachers should prepare achievement students well in advance about some of the ways in which judges pick winners for a competition. Competitors have to be as highly prepared as possible, but sometimes there are reasons a certain participant is chosen over another that aren't related to how the student played at all!

Achievement students criticize themselves to such an extent that criticism from a teacher can be like pouring salt on an open wound. Criticism needs to be given in the context of teaching. The best way to re-motivate a student after a discouraging event is to ask the student what they think needed improvement. You can help them develop an achievable plan to tackle these issues.

Inquisitiveness: The Need to Know (External)

Students who are always asking "Why?" are motivated by inquisitiveness. It's been noted that young children ask more than 100 questions a day, while adults ask around six questions a day. Curiosity is the main driver of learning, so being inquisitive will increase the motivation to learn. People who are motivated by inquisitiveness will naturally ask questions frequently, but this is such an important skill that I recommend trying to foster inquisitiveness in all students to whatever degree possible.

When even the most confident teacher encounters a student who is inquisitive, it's easy to feel that this student might be challenging authority and questioning directives. Au contraire! An inquisitive student will love digging deep and will learn faster when they understand why you are asking them to do something. For example:

Teacher: "Please keep your thumb bent on the bow."

Student: "Why?"

Teacher: "The thumb is the source of power in your tone."

Student: "How?"

Teacher: "Have you ever heard of Newton's third law? For every action, there is an equal and opposite reaction. Well, when your thumb pushes up, the fingers and arm relax downward to create tone."

Student: "How?"

Teacher: "Place your bow on the string in the middle of the bow. Now, push up with the thumb to create a reaction from the fingers and arm. See if you can make the stick and hair touch each other. Don't move the bow down and up, just keep it placed on the string. Can you make your bow stick do some push-ups by activating your thumb? Can you feel the reaction in the fingers?"

This exchange shows how an inquisitive student best functions in a learning situation. They need to draw out their own learning through questioning. Teachers can motivate inquisitive students by giving them the space to ask questions and find answers.

Ask lots of questions. When an inquisitive student isn't experienced at using their learning gifts, you might need to turn the tables and ask them a lot of questions yourself. Try not to ever tell them the answer—see if they can discover it! The Socrates method provides optimal learning with this type of student. Questions and more questions!

Take time to answer every question. It's interesting to notice how many times we ignore questions from kids. When we ignore a student's question, we are training them to be less curious. We already know that they'll ask fewer and fewer questions as they age. We should try to reduce this downward spiral as much as possible.

It's important for me to model a spirit of learning for my students. I shared earlier that when I noticed I was ignoring my own internal questions and started looking up answers, my inquisitiveness was jump-started after years of being fairly dormant. I've kept up this practice as much as possible, but when my schedule gets overloaded, my inquisitiveness suffers. Imagine how a student's schedule impacts their ability to stay inquisitive and also keep learning. A four-year-old has a less busy schedule, with plenty of time to ask questions and absorb new learning like a sponge. As a child gets older, they have more activities and less time to be curious. Consequently, learning slows. This is another reason to encourage

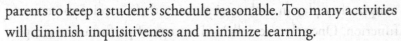

parents to keep a student's schedule reasonable. Too many activities will diminish inquisitiveness and minimize learning.

Assign research projects. How many times have we, as teachers, observed a masterclass with a prominent guest artist and listened to the deafening silence when the student is asked the poignant question "What does this word mean?" as the guest artist points to some elusive Italian word (leggiero, molto meno, piu mosso) in the student's music.

When I saw this happen to a student in a masterclass nearly 30 years ago, I vowed this would never occur with one of my students. So, whether they are inquisitive or not, they still have to look up every single word in their music—the inquisitive ones just enjoy it more! I expect this scholarly approach to repertoire as soon as descriptive words start appearing in the music. Even if the student doesn't read music very well, they can still see the word in the score, find out what it means, learn where it is in the piece, and apply its meaning to the music. These research projects can be applied to historical information about the piece, the time period, and the circumstances surrounding the piece being composed. I'm always pleasantly surprised by the delight I see in the eyes of an inquisitive student who has been assigned a research project related to their repertoire.

The tempo for a piece can vary between performers, and the indicated tempo on the printed music can be inaccurate. The student can listen to a variety of performers and write down the tempos they play in each section using their "tap in" metronome function. Once they've collected a range of performance tempos, they can pick a moderate tempo that fits their interpretation and stays within the acceptable tempo range for the piece.

Let their interests guide the lesson. Inquisitive students often present what seems like a lot of tangents. Just like it's important to answer all of the questions the inquisitive student asks, be sure to take the detours and tangents your student finds interesting. This is how you will motivate them to practice. I can teach someone to play a fantastic string crossing just as well using Vivaldi or Boil Them Cabbage Down. If a student gets interested in fiddle music, give them fiddle music. If they are excited by playing a tune from a movie, use it to help them with accidentals. Hedwig's Theme from Harry Potter and The Imperial March from Star Wars have introduced many students to complicated, interesting melodies that stretch their ears and playing skills.

During the years I home-schooled my kids, I enjoyed the writings and philosophy of Charlotte Mason. She said, "What a child digs for becomes his own possession." The deepest learning always occurs when the emotional centers of joy and pleasure are also activated. A student who is playing a piece they love will make this music their own possession!

Establish a "Question of the Week." You can inspire curiosity in all of your students by hanging up interesting pictures and then posing a question. For example, I posted a photo of a gymnast, carefully balanced on a balance beam, outside my studio door where students waited for the lesson time to begin. Under the photo, I posed this question: "What does this have to do with violin or viola playing?"

I was blown away by the diversity in the answers I got from my students. Here are a few of the answers my students gave:

- It's about keeping your bow on the bow path.
- It's about balancing your body weight on both feet for the most freedom.
- It's about shifting smoothly with no bumps.
- It's about the discipline needed to stay on course.

What was even more amazing was how each student's answer was almost always directly related to the concept they most needed to perfect or were currently working on.

Autonomy: The Need to Be Independent (Internal)

While the inquisitive student will often be inspired to work on their own by an external source, students motivated by autonomy like to work independently, regardless of assignments given by the teacher. This can be a blessing or a curse to the teacher. Most of the time, these students are very self-motivated when they are interested. However, the most headstrong do-it-yourselfers can get in the way of their own learning by refusing to accept instruction and deciding to do their own thing. With these students, the teacher has to balance authoritative directions with fostering a cooperative spirit. When a student feels ownership of an idea (even if you guided them toward it), it's likely to succeed with flying colors.

Assign planning tasks. Any student who wants to work independently needs to have good planning skills. The student should have a basic outline of what to plan each week for their practice sessions. The outline should include:

- What will be practiced (what piece and, specifically, what problem area or technical issue will be worked on during the practice segment)
- How it will be practiced (what methods)
- How long it will be practiced

I have a standard lesson assignment page that I fill out during the lesson with specific items to be worked on throughout the week. This can be used as a checklist for each practice session with any student. With autonomy students, I will often ask for even more detailed records of how they practiced. This gives them freedom to develop their own practice systems but allows me to assist them in tweaking these systems to be as effective as possible. Planning tasks can also apply to recital programs, house concerts, and developing special performances. Any opportunity to make and execute a plan is very motivating for autonomy students.

Offer choices in repertoire. Autonomy students want the freedom of making choices. When it's time to learn a new piece, offer several choices. I have one delightfully autonomous student who was selecting her next showpiece. I gave her no less than eight possible pieces from which to choose. After listening to all of them, she sent me a text asking for some further suggestions, since none of the original eight pieces had struck her fancy. She found a piece she really liked in the next set of eight pieces I sent her way, but she also increased her knowledge of violin showpieces immensely through this listening project. When it came time for the next piece to be selected, she already knew what she wanted to play.

One of my very wise teachers once said, "There are so many pieces in the violin repertoire. A student shouldn't play something they don't like." There's nothing that will stop a student's motivation quicker than stalling out on a challenging piece they don't like. Part of our job as their teacher is to find repertoire they like to play in order to keep their technique moving forward. There's no wisdom in forcing a student to learn a piece for their own good and consequently making them hate practicing and even contemplate quitting the instrument. As teachers, we need to be flexible with repertoire until the student self-identifies as a musician. Until that time, keep motivation at the forefront of your teaching agenda. Without it, the student won't progress. They won't be practicing, so they'll feel incompetent, which will make them not want to practice, which will make them more and more incompetent. It's a vicious circle.

Let students guide the lesson. With inquisitive students, letting the student guide the lesson is about following their tangents, even when they stray from what you had planned. For students motivated by autonomy, guiding the lesson is a more structured process. I have a certain order I use when I'm teaching a typical lesson. First, scales and arpeggios, followed by etudes and exercises. Next, we will work on the newest repertoire, and then finish the lesson with whatever piece is further along in the learning process.

However, with a student who is motivated by autonomy, I will often set up a back-and-forth system of selecting the lesson order. The student will pick what we work on first, I get to choose the second item, and so on. In this way, the student can guide the lesson, but I make sure we touch on the most important aspects of the lesson assignments. Earlier in my teaching career, I would allow students to completely choose the lesson order, until I realized they were avoiding certain things they felt unprepared to play or just didn't like to practice. By sharing the responsibility of selecting the lesson order, the autonomous student gets to choose some things but isn't allowed to avoid important tasks to their own detriment.

Encourage appropriate parental involvement. With the autonomous student, an overbearing parent can cause the focus of the daily practice to be on who is in control rather than how and what to practice. Over the years, I have had private meetings with several parents to talk to them about their child's motivational style and how to encourage them to use their child's desire for autonomy to their advantage. If the student's phase of development means that a parent is still involved in the practice sessions, parents can still offer autonomy. As the student practices, the parent can check in with the student periodically and let them demonstrate the product of what they've worked on. Together, they can review the student's plan for the next practice segment. The parent then repeats the process by returning between segments, hearing the student's progress, and planning for the upcoming practice period.

Allow students to guide the teaching. Although this can be trouble if it's overused, allowing the student to tell the teacher what they want to learn is fabulous. I've seen this used frequently in masterclass settings. The guest artist will ask, "What do you want to get better at?" or "What do you want to work on?" For the autonomous student, this question is a dream come true. As long as it's not used exclusively, the student will make great progress, because they are explicitly asking to learn something they are interested in learning.

Let's Stay Motivated!

Whether you're working in a classroom or with individual students, activating these eight motivators while mitigating as many of the roadblocks as possible takes careful thought—but the results are well worth the effort! Understanding your own motivational styles, as well as what motivates your students, helps you analyze your studio experience to identify any holes in the motivation landscape. Students with every motivational style can stay engaged and keep practicing, if we as teachers think creatively about adding any missing ingredients to our studio culture. These motivators give a teacher specific tools to unlock each child's excitement about learning. Once a child is engaged, the learning becomes much easier.

Every teacher has to be good at two things: the actual teaching of the material in their field and connecting with the student psychologically. The teacher must be both instructor and motivator. The tricky part is that practicing happens at home. Teachers aren't there to make sure it's a pleasant experience or ensure that the environment is truly motivating for students. Teachers have to create solid motivation in the studio so it carries over throughout the week and results in practicing at home!

If roadblocks to motivation have been removed, and the student has been armed with effective practice tools that speak to their own motivational styles, the results of successful practice will give the student that good feeling we all hope for. At this point, the brilliance of Thorndike's Law of Effect begins to take hold.

As the student practices more, another one of Thorndike's discoveries, the Law of Exercise from *Animal Intelligence* also comes into play.

Any response to a situation will, other things being equal, be more strongly connected with the situation in proportion to the number of times it has been connected with that situation and to the average vigor and duration of the connections.

In other words, the more my students practice or repeat something, the more likely they are to remember it. The Law of Effect and the Law of Exercise are completely intertwined when it comes to student success. If my students have the tools to make practice sessions successful, they will likely enjoy playing their instruments more (Law of Effect). Because they enjoy playing their instruments, they will practice more (Law of Exercise). This is the essence of learning.

Motivation is the special ingredient that makes the process of learning easier. A student's reserve of this special ingredient can be increased by using tools that match the student's motivational style. The ideas in this book have helped me motivate many of my students. I hope they also help you boost your students' motivation and musicianship.

In other words, the more my students practice or repeat something, the more likely they are to remember it. The Law of Effect and the Law of Exercise are completely intertwined when it comes to student success. If my students have the tools to make practice sessions successful, they will likely enjoy playing their instruments more (Law of Effect). Because they enjoy playing their instruments, they will practice more (Law of Exercise). This is the essence of learning.

Motivation is the special ingredient that makes the process of learning easier. A student's desire of this special ingredient can be increased by using tools that match the student's motivational style. The ideas in this book have helped me motivate many of my students. I hope they also help you boost your students' motivation and musicianship.

APPENDIX

Coyle, Daniel (2009). *The Talent Code: Greatness Isn't Born. It's Grown. Here's How.* Bantam.

Deci, Edward L. and Richard M. Ryan (1985). *Intrinsic Motivation and Self-Determination in Human Behavior (Perspectives in Social Psychology).* Plenum Press.

Gregory, Gayle and Martha Kaufeldt (2015). *The Motivated Brain: Improving Student Attention, Engagement, and Perseverance.* ASCD.

Knowledge Is Power Program. kipp.org.

Lavoie, Richard (2007). *The Motivation Breakthrough: 6 Secrets to Turning On the Tuned-Out Child.* Touchstone.

Thorndike, Edward (1911). *Animal Intelligence: Experimental Studies.* The Macmillan Company.

ABOUT THE AUTHOR

Ruth Meints is the Executive Director of the Omaha Conservatory of Music, where she also maintains a violin and viola studio. She conducts various workshops around the country in violin/ viola pedagogy, motivation and learning styles, integrating current neuroscience findings into music teaching. She authored the five-year String Sprouts curriculum, with the Conservatory's program currently enrolling over one thousand preschoolers from underserved areas at no cost to the families. Her teaching experience has included head of the string department at Azusa Pacific University, faculty at Biola University in the Los Angeles area, violin/viola instructor at University of Nebraska-Omaha, as well as faculty at San Jose Talent Education and Omaha Talent Education. In 2016, Ruth was given the Governor's Arts Award for excellence in arts education sponsored by Nebraska Arts Council and Nebraska Cultural Endowment. She has also presented a TedXOmaha talk entitled "Music, Preschoolers, and Poverty."

ABOUT STRING SPROUTS

In 2013, the Omaha Conservatory of Music launched an innovative new program called String Sprouts aimed at creating equitable access to the arts for young children growing up in under-resourced areas. The curriculum, authored by Ruth Meints, is based on foundational tenets from both the Suzuki and the El Sistema philosophies. Children enroll in the program at 3 and 4-years-old and caregiver involvement is mandatory. Instruments are provided for each student at no cost to the families for all five years of the program. The group class lessons are held exclusively in underserved areas. It's a community-wide initiative to give all children the opportunity to learn a stringed instrument with a ready-to-use curriculum and engaging new repertoire by composer Dryden Meints. (String Odyssey available at meintsproductions.com)

In 2020, the Omaha Conservatory's String Sprouts program enrolled over 1,300 children and continues to grow. Program evaluation has shown positive results in improving school-readiness skills and developing stronger family relationships. As the famous cellist Pablo Casals once said, "Music will save the world." String Sprouts is an extraordinary journey that moves the world one step closer to making this dream a reality.

If you would like more information about how to start your own String Sprouts program or register for String Sprouts teacher training courses, please contact the Omaha Conservatory at www.stringsprouts.org

CPSIA information can be obtained
at www.ICGtesting.com
Printed in the USA
LVHW041104100722
723138LV00005B/394